Enough Already!

**Library of Congress
Cataloging-in-Publication Data**

Magee, Jeffrey L., Ph.D., CMC, PDM
Enough Already: 50 immediate ways to deal with,
manage & eliminate negativity at work or home /
Jeffrey L. Magee

Spaith, Nancey, editor
Weems, Jim, graphic design and layout

© 1998 by, JEFF MAGEE INTERNATIONAL / JMI®
JMI® Publishing Group

P.O. Box 701918
Tulsa, OK, 74170-1918
Tollfree at 1-877-90-MAGEE

ISBN: 0-9641240-9-2

Enough Already!

Jeff Magee, Ph.D./CMC

 **50** fast ways to deal with, manage and eliminate **negativity** at work or home.

Enough Already!

Have you ever noticed when you seem to be really, really in a good mood and things seem to really be going great, there always seems to be someone or something that just must pull you down? Well...

Enough already!

So you feel that dealing with negativity and negative people should be less stressful than it appears. Well...

Enough already!

There are some very simple and immediate interaction techniques for dealing with negative situations, negative people and just negativity in general. So...

Enough already!

Here are the 50 fastest ways to turn a negative person or negative situation around, when you feel like...

Enough already!

And, if that isn't reason enough to commit to changing a negative person or situation into a productive encounter, consider the basic mathematics of how much down time associated with negativity you have had in the past year.

> ❏ **Assessment One:** How much mental (and/or possibly physical) time do you spend reflecting on negative things, situations or people when they arise? _____ (seconds or minutes per typical reflection)!

> ❏ **Assessment Two:** How many times a day might such a down time occur? _____!

> ❏ **Assessment Three:** Now multiply the number in Assessment One times the number in Assessment Two: _____ !
> This number now represents how much time, on average, you spend (or waste) each day bogged down in negative matters.

If this number isn't alarming enough, then consider multiplying the number in Assessment Three times the number of days in the year. What a quick reality check on the amount of time wasted on negative thoughts, situations, and people – thus holding one back from success. Isn't that...

Enough already!

"Nothing in the world will take the place of persistence.

Talent will not; nothing is more common than unsuccessful men with talent.

Genius will not; unrewarded genius is almost a proverb.

Education will not; the world is full of educated derelicts.

Persistence and determination alone are omnipotent.

The slogan 'Press on' has solved and always will solve the problems of the human race."

– Calvin Coolidge

• • • • •

With the right techniques you can "Press on" and learn how to deal with, manage and even eliminate negativity at work and home.

Enough already!

Here then are the 50 fastest techniques for dealing with, managing and even eliminating negativity at work and at home.

So "Press on" and if one technique doesn't work, then smile with the thought that your back-up action plans are countless in number and powerful in scope

Enough already!

Contents

• • • • •

Avoidance:
The Liassez-Faire Management Approach

If only it were this simple, your problems would be done!

How many times when you were growing up did you hear your parents tell you, just avoid the thing that causes your negativity.

Isn't it interesting that, while we heard this simple approach to negativity, we were unable to hold back and just had to put our nose in where it didn't belong.

Technique #1 – AVOIDANCE – is simple!

Avoid both people and situations which you know will end in negativity. The action step here is simple; avoid those people or situations that aren't a must for you to pursue and which you know will only end in negativity.

They aren't winning by us conceding. We are winning by not engaging! Channel all of those energies toward a constructive task or objective.

Don't Argue

H ave you noticed that when you get pulled into a conversation with a negative person, it can quickly escalate into a debate and then a full blown argument.

And to make the situation even more negative, the more you argue with negative people, the more energy they seem to gain and the more exhausted you become?

Is that true for you?

It's as though you are a gas station for them. They come up to you, plug in, pull all your energy out and go onto the next person. You are left exhausted and dead!

Technique #2 – DON'T ARGUE.

Negative people have been playing the argument and debate game all of their lives and are masters of the argument. No matter how well you can debate, there is no victory here, as tempers will flare and emotion will burst out between the combatants. The action plan here:

First, let the arguer vent 100 percent. They are not expecting this. And by all means, don't interrupt them, as this is what they expect.

Second, to ensure that you don't interrupt them or get pulled into the argument, your mouth needs something to do. It is typically your mouth that gets you into trouble with negative people. So, while you let them vent, you take notes. That's right, take non-combative notes. This will help you track the essential elements of the conversation that the other person feels are critical for discussion, and it will ensure that your mouth stays shut!

You can't talk and take coherent notes at the same time. Now, hold them accountable for what you have written and talk through each point, one at a time!

Isolation

The simple point here is to limit your exposure to these people and limit their exposure to you. You're not giving in here and they are not outsmarting you. Remember the old statement, "out of sight, out of mind!"

Technique #3 – ISOLATION. Limiting your exposure to the person who appears to push your buttons!

Don't go out of your way to avoid them. Consider your options prior to engagement. Recognize that there may be another route in the office or home you can take to get from where you are to where you need to be, and take it. Thus limit your exposure to the negative person.

Limiting your exposure can also mean putting yourself into environments whereby you limit your odds of coming into routine contact with them. Limit eye contact, sitting, and interaction that is not essential. This will begin to reduce the tension and negativity (or perceived negativity) between the two of you.

If you're in management, this could mean limiting the interaction of two productive individuals, who, when placed together, become negative and combatant toward one another.

Garner Support Before

Sociologists tell us that whenever you interact with a group of individuals, the dynamics will be such that the group will break down into three distinct subgroups.

One of the subgroups will be composed of the followers who are neutral to any issue and will merely join forces with the subgroup that influences them first or most. This group of followers is the bulk of the larger group. Some experts estimate reflecting that as many as 80 percent of any group are followers of the influencers.

The other subgroups are the two that influence the dynamics of the larger group – and each is initially balanced at about 10 percent of the larger group. One subgroup is the forward thinkers or transformers. The second influence subgroup is the resisters to anything and everything (or the terrorists of you).

Technique #4 – GARNER SUPPORT BEFORE you engage with others!

Always ask yourself, do I have a support nucleus or alliance base when I attempt to interact with others? This will reduce the number of times that a negative situation can develop and the number of times that a negative person (terrorist) will challenge you in front of others!

You can recruit supporters very easily. Ask yourself who in the larger group would support you because of who you are (friends, allies, people that owe you a favor) or who in the group has the most to gain from your proposition.

Always seek these individuals out prior to interacting with the group and present yourself/your ideas to them for their buy-in.

Suggest Ideas Be Written Down with a Rationale

Sometimes negative people just live for the opportunity to interrupt you, saying "that won't work" or bringing their problems to you with the expectation that you should assume their problems and resolve their work.

Technique #5 – SUGGEST THAT IDEAS BE WRITTEN DOWN. Before you engage in dialogue get a list with rationale for discussion!

The intent here is that when someone approaches you with a problem or interrupts you with a matter they wish to discuss which has nothing to do with what you are presently discussing, you could politely direct them, by saying,

> "That's a great point (or idea). If you would write that down, with a few of your ideas as to how we can proceed with it, we can get back together later and discuss it."

And then continue on with what you were discussing or doing prior to their interruption. Don't stare at them, don't make additional remarks. You have made your point, now move on!

Have Most Vocal Objectors State Positions First

Why wait anxiously for that negative person to ambush you or take a sniper shot at you from the sidelines? Change your approach and pull the group together (See GARNER SUPPORT BEFORE suggestion.) from the beginning. Smoke out any potential negative person and use peer pressure to your advantage.

> **Technique #6 – HAVE MOST VOCAL OBJECTOR STATE POSITION FIRST. Take the element of surprise away from the negative person and use it to your benefit!**

For example, if you know there are persons in the group who can derail your initiatives with negative comments, invite them to present their ideas first,

> "... some of you may have differing views, I would invite those for discussion, along with the merits of proceeding as I have just outlined."

Still the thunder from the opposition by calling for their remarks and rally peer pressure to your advantage.

If the opposition doesn't have some sound logic for differing views, it makes it even more difficult for them to offer their perspectives. What they are used to is interrupting you to state their objections. Then they sit back while you fall into the standard trap of defending your position or rejustifying your position. Now, you side-step all that grief with a controlled conversation! In essence, put up or shut up is what you are doing, without saying it!

Walk Away

Why do we even give negative people our time and attention?

Keep in mind that, without an audience, the negative person may change his actions and behavior to get attention. The only direction to change negative behavior is toward neutral or positive behavior!

Technique #7 – WALK AWAY. Don't give negative people your time or attention!

Enough said.

Seek Linkage and Compromise

Sometimes negativity arises due to an unwill-ingness by one or both parties to look at issues from all angles to determine if there may be some common points of interest.

When interacting with another person on a nega-tive subject, back up and examine the evidence, information, issues and true bottom line needs of all of the parties involved to determine what may be a common point of interest Keep in mind that *interest* means the motivator of one's needs or positions, and work together from that com-mon ground.

> *Technique #8 – SEEK LINKAGE AND COMPROMISE. Look for the common ground and focus conversation and energies toward that point!*

By looking for the mysterious thread called "com-mon ground" that runs between the two of you, you then have a reason to come together and put down your negativity to one another.

Don't Feed the Negaholic

Some people look for issues at work, at home, even on the drive from home to work and back again to complain about and be negative about.

Don't be a willing participant in this game of negativity. Don't provide them with information or issues to be negative about.

Technique #9 – DON'T FEED THE NEGAHOLIC. They are addicted to stuff (information, people, events, etc.) in order to get their fix!

Sometimes you run into people (Maybe they 're on your family tree.) who have been negative for as long as you can remember. No matter what you do, you can't change them.

That's the clue!

You can't change them, but you can change how you see them and how you choose to interact with them. And, most importantly, you can choose what you provide to them. Do we feed their need and fixations or do we help them to dry out?

Use Double Standards

Some people just don't get it!

Getting people to realize that what they see or hear as negative in one person, they may hear or see as acceptable in another, can be achieved by using double standards. Sometimes, what may trigger your negative internal feelings, may actually be a misunderstanding of reality and your own double standards.

> ### *Technique #10 – USE DOUBLE STANDARDS – to get people to realize that they are creating their own negativity by not being fair!*

Sometimes you hear a person say something that sounds rather assertive on your ear. Yet, when someone else makes the same statement, it doesn't sound assertive, yet rather over-assertive. If you don't hear *what* is being said, because of your distraction over *how* it is being said, then you have just experienced a double standard.

Example:

> ❑ A man says something in an assertive manner, you say he is assertive. If he communicates in an over assertive tone or

manner, you probably still say, that he is assertive or, perhaps, over-assertive.

❑ Yet, if a women communicates in an assertive manner you *may* say she is assertive. But, if she communicates in an over assertive tone or manner, more than likely you didn't even hear what she said, because of how she said it. You heard her as a b-i-t-c-h. True or false?

Consider the number of negative situations that have arisen due to double standards.

Take Responsibility

Negative people always seem to point their finger at others and blame others for their position in life.

Successful people point their fingers at themselves and take responsibility. On a television interview show, the successful individual being profiled says that the reason he is successful is because he took responsibility and did something.

And the "failure" on that same television show has an endless series of reasons and excuses for why he is not successful. The one thing you don't hear from him is that he is a failure because of something he did or did not do!

Technique #11 – TAKE RESPONSIBILITY. Do something!

The next time you find yourself cornered by the negative person or a negative situation, let it consume you by not doing something or take responsibility and make it disappear!

Do Cost-Benefit Analysis

Have you ever reflected back upon an inter-action with someone and reveled in your victory. Yet, because of the victory, now there is some negative tension between yourself and the individual you tramped over?

And, upon further reflection what you won seems to be less important today than it was at the height of the battle with the negative individual. And, at last it occurs to you that for all of the energy you invested in that earlier interaction, the outcome really was not worth all of the ef-fort, well that would be

Technique #12 – DO COST-BENEFIT ANALYSIS. Determine if the investment of costs will be worth the final benefit or outcome(s)!

Conduct a Time-and-Motion Study

Wow!

Think of the number of interactions that ended in increased stress, tension among individuals, and increased frustration on your feet. The next time you are about to connect with a negative person or work on a project that has the potential of becoming negative, ask yourself,

> "Is this even worth my time? For the amount of energy that it will take and the work involved, what are the real net results going to be."

Technique #13 – CONDUCT A TIME-AND-MOTION STUDY to determine if the interaction or endeavor is even worth your time!

Many of the places we put our energy in and people we interact with are just not worth it. In a classic line from the hit television program, *Frasier*, character Dr. Niles Crane says of a negative person he is interacting with,

"I am far too important and you are far too insignificant for me to be talking with!"

While a little blunt, it is very telling of what our time is truly worth!

Assign 100% Accountability

L ike clock-work, there always seems to be a negative person around to give you advise on how to do the things that you're working on. In meetings, it seems like there is always a negative person (terrorist) who chimes in and says there are better ways to proceed on your projects!

There are several ways here, to turn this negative, or potentially negative, situation into a powerfully positive outcome.

Technique #14 – ASSIGN 100% ACCOUNTABILITY – to the very person who has taken no responsibility but has all of the answers!

There are a few applications of this strategy: First, be prepared to turn over all aspects of a project to the other individual and walk away with a positive attitude. If he initiates his typical constructive feedback (as he likes to call it), then offer to let him assume the project and make sure his name appears on the bottom-line of accountability. Either he makes it happen and you win, with one less project. Or you win, he commits suicide on the project he thought he knew so much about!

A second way to proceed is if you know he has the potential to derail efforts with his nitpicking, put him in charge from the outset and make sure that he and only he is being held accountable for the bottom line. Don't assign a task to him _and_ someone else. If he doesn't like the other person, then he won't participate and he will blame the other person for any failures.

Stimulate Conversation

Most conversations with negative people seem to focus on the "why" of the subject matter. After a while, talking with a negative person is a little like trying to have a conversation with a child. Every time the child doesn't like what he hears or doesn't understand what is being said, that child instantly calls out a "why."

Typically the next person talking is the parent. Even before the parent has a clue as to what the child may really mean, the parent throws himself into the position of defending, representing or justifying what he has said.

When you find yourself at the receiving end of a negative person saying "why" to you, respond with a conversation starter.

Technique #15 – STIMULATE CONVERSATIONS – the way we were taught in grammar class!

You can always open a conversation in a non-combative manner with the other person by getting him to share his feelings or views on the:

Who
What
When
Where
Why
How

Demand Alternatives

Here it is, the single most powerful way to professionally and maturely interact with a person when the potential for negativity between the two of you is high. The single most powerful way to approach a negative person who always finds fault with what you say, is even more powerful when it can be done in the presence of others.

Technique #16 – DEMAND ALTERNATIVES – *every time a negative person finds fault with your ideas!*

This can be tricky, but when done correctly, it is powerful and devastating!

Rule of three: The best application of this technique is to be prepared to do it in multiple of threes. What we mean is this: When someone challenges you and says your plan or idea won't work, don't argue with them – they will be expecting this. Don't defend yourself – they will be expecting this. Don't challenge them – they will be expecting this.

How do you do this? Simple! Pretend you're a broken record. At the very instance the negative person challenges or interrupts you with his standard, "that won't work" statement, respond with a calm, cool tone of voice and say,

"if this won't work, what do you feel we should do?"

If he doesn't respond with a tangible, and says, "I don't know," then you immediately follow up with the exact same question to him. And, if on the second attempt at conversation, he can't put up, then you perform the same drill a third time. Notice that everyone will be watching and listening. If the other person can't produce a tangible response by the third time, don't go for a fourth. Merely continue with the dialogue at the point where you were initially interrupted and notice that the negative person will not interrupt you again.

Peer pressure is working with you and all three subgroups will unite as one, and unite behind you!

If the other person should, at one of your three questions to him, actually respond with an answer, never discuss it or pass judgment on it at the precise time that it is offered. Instead, require that he expand on his response so that you have time to better evaluate their response for viability or ineffectiveness.

Technique #17 – DEMAND ALTERNATIVES – ask WHY if he offers any response to your questions!

Just as a child would do to an adult when the adult says something that the child either disagrees with or doesn't like, that child immediately turns to the adult and says,

"why do you say that" or "tell me more about that idea."

Get the negative person to open up and explain his comment for better discussion or get him to rescind his remarks by asking him politely to expand.

Enough Already!

Utilize Ownership Words

To reduce the escalation of tension and negativity between individuals, the conversation should contain non-combative language or ownership vocabulary. Both in print and in oral communications, the language should always be directed back toward yourself and not at the other person.

Technique #18 – UTILIZE OWNERSHIP WORDS. These words, when strung together, imply the finger is pointing back toward yourself!

Ownership words are words like:

We
Us
I
Feel
Team

· **Avoid Challenge Words**

To reduce the escalation of tension and negativity between individuals, the conversation
should contain non-combative language or avoid
the tendency to use challenge vocabulary. Both
in print and in oral communications, the language should always be directed back toward
yourself and not at the other person.

> **Technique #19 – AVOID CHALLENGE
> WORDS. These words, when strung
> together, imply the finger
> is pointing back at the other person!**

Challenge words sound and look like:

> However
> You
> But
> And
> Think
> Opinion
> No
> Because

Challenge words typically stimulate one's emotions. Once emotions are stimulated the
likelihood of clear and rational thinking goes

down greatly. Some professions even train their members to use challenge words to throw their audience off guard.

Focus when you talk, write, and work to avoid the words that distract the other person. Work to keep yourself and others focused on what really matters, and watch negativity decrease!

A + *B* = C

Psychology offers a lot of interesting theories and great techniques for dealing with negative people and situations for more positive outcome. One of the hallmarks of the theories lies in a model constructed in the 1950s by Dr. Albert Ellis, the father of Rational Emotive Behavior Therapy (REBT).

The model which came to be known as the *ABC Model to Human Behavior* says:

> ❑ In life there will always be "A" and "C" factors. All that an individual has control over is the "B."

> ❑ If one doesn't like the "A" or the "C," then focus energies on the "B." Don't get distracted by the "A" or the "C." It is the "A" merged with our "B" that makes up the "C" in life which we experience.

The "B" represents the *behavior* that one exhibits when dealt an "A" in life. The "A" represents the *activating events* in life which we encounter (and everything is an activating event in one manner or another). And, the "C" represents the *consequences* which are a result of how we encounter the activating events and what we do when merged.

Technique #20 – A+B=C – encourages you to focus your energy on your own Behavior!

Negativity and negative people are born out of attempts to change either the "A" or the "C" which is impossible. An "A" is history and the "C" has just occurred. If you don't like either the "A" or the "C" then decide what you can do differently next time when you encounter the "A," so that you can arrive at a different "C!"

Empathy

S ome people make things difficult and some people seem to make a lot of noise just getting noticed. In their defense, this may be the behavior that they learned early in life to get attention.

The next time someone yells or raises his voice at you, don't let that be the trigger to negativity. Instead, empathize with him, as this can become a great diffuser to others' negativity.

Technique #21 – EMPATHY.
Acknowledge the other person!

Empathizing with the other person does not imply that you are agreeing with him, nor does it mean that he is correct in his views. It merely means that you have heard him and acknowledge his statement.

Some people feel that they have to become negative and raise their voice before others will even recognize them – now you bypass all of the hostility and tension can borne negativity at home and work!

Seek Consensus With SMART©

Think of the number of times you have left an interaction with a mental understanding of what you and the other person have agreed to do. When you come back together, you find that you were more committed than they, and because of that commitment (or lack of), the two of you are now engaged in negativity and conflict with one another over the agreed-upon issue.

The professional training industry teaches a communication agreement technique, called SMART© that will enable you to maintain a controlled conversation with the other party (over the telephone, in writing, or face-to-face) and work towards a clear understanding between all parties before parting with one another.

Technique #22 – SMART.
Use this approach to seek consensus!

Conversationally, you are working to **attain agreement** to the letters, S, M, R, and T. What you are doing is the letter **A**. Each letter represents a conversational step that needs to be clearly addressed and understood by both parties in order to reach a higher level of consensus (commitment). The letters represent:

❑ **S = Specific**. Be as specific as necessary with the other party. Specific is dealing with WHAT you are discussing!

❑ **M = Measurable**. Make sure you discuss in detail the acceptable action steps for progress. Measurable deals with HOW one is to proceed, or the HOW we are going to do this factor!

❑ **R = Realistic.** If the other party doesn't feel that what is being discussed is realistic or reachable, he is not going to commit 100 percent of his energies toward it. And, in fact, this may be the very reason that he became negative (a terrorist). Realistic will be speaking to the WHY of the matter. WHY we must do something, or WHY we must stop something, etc.

❑ **T = Time-frame.** Be as specific as necessary with the deadline window or WHEN it is needed.

If something needs to be done by the end of the day, don't say, "I need this by the end of today." That is a vague time-frame and can lead to negativity if your interpretation of end of the day is 5 P.M. and the other person thought it was 4:30 P.M. or 5:30 P.M. Be very clear on the time-frames.

The SMART© formula gives you a tracking device to counter known potential negatives that can arise from miscommunication.

To underscore the value of this technique, consider the number of times you have experienced negativity or conflict due to being at the receiving end of one of these responses (excuses) for non performance:

❑ "Oh, I am sorry, I didn't realize that is WHAT you wanted!"

❑ "Oh, I am sorry, I didn't realize I could do it that way (HOW) or use that to do this!"

❑ "It wasn't realistic to get it done, with everything else I had to do!" (They missed the magnitude of the WHY when you initially communicated to them!)

❑ "Oh, I didn't realize that you needed it right now (WHEN)." Or, "Oh, I am sorry, I didn't realize WHEN you asked for it, that you meant you needed it right now!"

Wow. Great conversational guide posts.

The place we heard (and learned) these responses (or excuses) first was in our homes from the others that live with us. Once we perfected them, we were ready for an employer to hire us so we could try them out on others and give them some negativity to deal with!

Enough Already!

Use an
ACTION MEMO©

Has it become a norm on the planet for people to be able to identify every problem known, but be incapable of brainstorming solutions or action plans to solve those problems? Why are the individuals capable of identifying the problems and challenges (and in great detail) unable to incorporate the positive with the negative?

Enter a conversational approach that can be accomplished orally or visually (You don't actually have to create a memo document).

Technique #23 – ACTION MEMO©. Use this approach to facilitate interactions and move quickly from problem identification to solution orientation!

The Action Memo© requires that conversation and brain power be applied to only two factors. First, complete identification and communication of WHAT the subject matter is. And, second, development of HOW to proceed, given the WHAT factor.

The next time someone brings his crises or "wild fires" to you for the magical work that you seem capable of, turn the conversation back to him and assist him in cultivating several HOW to's for the WHAT factor.

Go One-on-One in Private

When all else fails, it might be time for a little one-on-one interaction with your negaholic in private. Remember, the power of in private is that there are no witnesses and you will be able to focus on the two of you and not on who may be listening or watching!

Once in private, you can work to determine what you or others may have done to precipitate their negativity, and, if in fact you did something, only when the root source of the negativity is determined, can you begin to work to rebuild the relationship.

> ***Technique #24 – GO ONE-ON-ONE IN PRIVATE. If all else fails attempt to find out why there seems to be such difficulty and negativity between the two of you.***

The purpose of this one-on-one private interaction is two-fold. First, is the obvious meeting of the minds and attempting to find resolution to the problems between you, thus downing the negativity. The second reason for this private interaction is ground work for any future public one-on-one interactions which may escalate, due to unsuccessful private interactions.

Go One-on-One in Public

So you have tried a lot of these techniques (and others) and even attempted to reach a meeting of the mind in a private one-on-one interaction. Don't give up hope. There are still a lot of techniques that await your deployment!

Some negative people live for the public showdown. While common sense dictates that you don't want to go here, there may be a specific time when this is the exact medicine for them. A word of caution, be very careful, controlled, focused, and non emotional!

Technique #25 – GO ONE-ON-ONE IN PUBLIC. If all else fails and your attempts for mature, professional resolution in private encounters has failed to produce any change in behavior, no matter how hard you try, go public!

Your approach is very clear. The other person has been dogged about being negative in your presence. You have talked to yourself a million times on your drive home or to work about that person and how one day you are going to stop taking this negativity. Let that emotion out during those private times, as that is not what you want to communicate when you do finally reach that point where you feel that you must go one-on-one in public with them.

So what do you do? Simple:

❏ **Step One – THE OPENING.** Your opening comments must be directed to all of the witnesses and not at the negative person (negaholic or terrorist). You want your opening remarks to set a powerful stage from which you can pull the others to your side. You want to have peer pressure working with you, assisting in putting weight behind your words.

An example of an OPENING line may sound like this, "Jeff, you and I have discussed this in private and in fact when we discussed this on last Thursday, we agreed that _____ (insert what the two of you agreed upon as your course of mature interaction for future interactions). I am not going to participate in this conversation."

Now you immediately move to step TWO. Don't get bogged down in debate and don't hesitate, which could give the other person an opportunity to interrupt your flow. Move from Step One to Step Two and through to Step Three and then get out of that environment!

❏ **Step Two – THE BODY.** Your focus needs to be to quickly set the stage for the witnesses benefit, and then get to the

BODY. This is where you say your piece. This is where you address the subject matter in your rational view. Be careful to not talk too long here. Get to the point and move on to the final step, Step Three!

Most people will talk about this technique, GO ONE-ON-ONE IN PUBLIC, but very few will ever do this. That may be exactly why a perceived level of negativity persists in their lives.

❑ **Step Three – THE CLOSE.** This is the step that few remember for their one-on-one interactions. Typically, effort is put into how to start our conversation and what we want to say, but little to no time is invested on the best way to terminate a conversation – how to shut up powerfully!

A way to move from Step One through the next two steps might sound like, "We agreed that, if you don't like my ideas, you would come to me in private to discuss your disagreement, instead of talking about one another behind the other's back. And I agreed to listen objectively to you. Now, you have decided to violate even that agreement. If you have something to say, then I will be willing to listen in the other room. Otherwise, drop it!"

Immediately turn and walk toward the other room. If he makes a sniper-shot comment towards you as you walk away, DO NOT STOP AND ENGAGE IN DEBATE WITH HIM as that is what he wants (and has been perfecting all of his life).

Oops Management: Admit Mistakes

Negative situations typically arise from mistakes or perceived mistakes. Negative people love to catch others in the act of the mistake or the cover-up.

The more work put into hiding, covering up, ignoring or denying a mistake merely escalates the negativity.

Technique #26 – OOPS MANAGEMENT: ADMIT MISTAKES move on!

To reduce or even eliminate any degree of negativity that could be associated with a mistake, admit the mistake at the earliest opportunity and as loudly as appropriate. This takes all of the fun away from the negative people who would otherwise enjoyed making your mistake public news. Now, all energies can be applied to the resolution and moving forward!

Write It Down

Negative situations have a tendency to escalate in conversations when your hands have nothing to do. For that reason, you need a mechanism to keep control of your physical body, so that you don't escalate a negative situation into a full-blown conflict.

Usually, when a negative situation develops one or both parties engage in the discussion, starts gesturing at the other to reinforce key spoken words. Unfortunately, this is usually taken in a threatening way and escalates the negativity.

Technique #27 – WRITE IT DOWN.
Keep a piece of paper nearby for
conversations with hard-core negative
people so you can take notes while
they talk. Keep your hands from
interrupting them or pointing at
them! And move on!

In a non-threatening manner, while the other person is talking, you take notes. It is impossible for your mouth to move, interrupting him and for your fingers to cut him off if you are concentrating on listening and taking notes. The notes also serve to assist in tracking the essential elements of the conversation from the negative person's perspective, allowing you to address each point when he finishes talking.

Also, by taking the notes you won't feel as compelled to interrupt. Without interrupting the other person, you're not giving him a reason to escalate the negativity.

When the two of you part company, you can throw the notes away if appropriate. The mere fact that you took the notes meant that you were in more control of yourself and managed the dynamic differently than previous interactions.

Ask a Negative Question

Negative people love to ask negative questions. Why should they have all of the fun?

Next time you say something or present an idea to others, make as a negative question, a part of your remarks.

Technique #28 – ASK A NEGATIVE QUESTION!

Still the thunder from the negative person and reduce, perhaps even eliminate, a negative situation, by posing the negative question. It might sound like this,

> ❏ "Given what I have just said and presented, there may in fact be some reasons to not do this and or do something else. So let me ask that question of us first, before we explore the merits of what I have just presented?"

Enough Said

S ometimes it's a matter of talking too much and inviting the negative person and negative situations to come your direction.

"Know when to hold them and know when to fold them" as Kenny Rogers says in the *Gambler*. The same holds true for talking. Know when to talk and know when it is best to know when enough has been said.

Technique #29 – ENOUGH SAID. Know when to shut up and walk away!

Enough said. Enough already!

Enough Done

Sometimes no matter how much you do isn't enough for the negative person. And, no matter how hard you work, the other person never seems to be pleased. So, know when enough has been done.

Technique #30 – ENOUGH DONE. Know when it's time to walk away!

Have you noticed that some of the stress, tension and anxiety that you experience may be associated with the very activities and events that you have actually volunteered for?

That may be a powerful clue. Why volunteer for negativity? STOP it!

Be Sensitive to the "Relationship Teeter-Totter©"

E very interaction impacts the degree of relationship which is, or is not, present between
you and the other party. In <u>YIELD MANAGE-
MENT</u>© by CRC PRESS/St. Lucie Press (by Jeff
Magee, ©, 1998), the idea of an always-present
relationship teeter-totter between people
(whether in personal or professional relations),
was put forth as well as the idea that it is our
actions that either reinforce the positive relationship or our actions which detract from the
relations was put forth.

*Technique #31 – BE SENSITIVE TO THE
"RELATIONSHIP TEETER-TOTTER©."
Ensure you put your actions into the
deposit side!*

If you visualize a relationship like a teeter-totter, then you can see that one side of the balance
beam is the positive side (the deposits one makes
into the relationship) and the other side of the
balance beam is the negative (or the degree of
withdrawals being made from the relationship).

Many times negativity stems from someone making too many withdrawals. The teeter-totter falls too much in the negative direction.

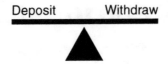

Deposit   Withdraw

When you talk or interact with someone on issues that have the potential to turn negative, or with an individual who has the ability to turn negative, visualize that relationship as a teeter-totter and ask yourself if your actions are adding to the positive side or negative side?

This gives you significant insight into which way the other person will direct the conversation and his action.

Turn Off the Negative "Inner Voice Dialogue©"

Sometimes, listening to the negative inner voice that talks to you about a situation or person, associated with negativity causes the most negativity for you.

Once that voice is activated, like clock-work we engage in a negative "Inner Voice Dialogue©" with it. The more you talk to yourself, the more the negativity increases!

In *POWER CHARGED FOR LIFE©* by JMI Publishing (by Jeff Magee, ©, 1994), the concept of our negative internal voice was put forth.

Technique #32 – TURN OFF THE NEGATIVE "INNER VOICE DIALOGUE©." Switch your inner voice discussion or dialogue to a more positive target!

The purpose of this technique is to cue yourself when you go negative and switch your internal voice from that negative "Inner Voice Dialogue©" to a positive inner voice!

Reframe

With the proper internal positive voice, you can reframe a situation or person. Instead of thinking about the state of negativity you are in, transfer your thoughts to anything that is more positive.

Technique #33 – REFRAME – your thoughts and how you see the facts and evidence leading to your negative state of mind!!

Look at the incident which got you to the negative state of mind. Examine it from another vantage point or different perspective. Reframe your thinking. Attempt to see the other side.

Break the Cycle of Negative Phrase Norms

Sometimes negativity comes out of the constant use of negative words or sayings. Break the cycle by using positive words or phrases. When you hear others using negatively charged words or phrases, move to make them sound more positive.

Technique #34 – BREAK THE CYCLE OF NEGATIVE PHRASE NORMS. Say things in a way that gives unity and hope to others!

Move from negative sayings to positive or option oriented sayings. Give hope to yourself and others, not disparity.

Negative phrases/words	Positive phrases/words
❏ No	❏ Perhaps
❏ Problems	❏ Possibilities/ opportunities
❏ You	❏ Us/we/team

- ❏ It must be someone's fault
- ❏ Let's examine the facts

- ❏ I can't
- ❏ I can/we can/ let's explore

- ❏ I think
- ❏ My feelings on this are...

- ❏ That's not my area
- ❏ I may not know, let's look...

- ❏ Don't mess that up...
- ❏ Would you like my assistance...

By investing a few seconds to rephrase a statement, you can break out of the phrasing that may actually be adding to or causing negativity in your life!

Use STOP©
to Stop Negative
Conversations

When confronted with negativity; most people can get bogged down in the discussion of what the problem is or the multitude of reasons why it is a problem. The problem here is that the more time spent on talking about what the issue is or why it is the issue, nothing gets done!

So the need for a systematic conversational technique to focus energies away from one another, from getting bogged down in the endless discussion on what the issue is and why it is the issue, becomes ever more necessary.

Technique #35 – USE STOP© TO STOP NEGATIVE CONVERSATIONS. Make them solution conversations instead!

STOP© becomes a decision model and technique that can aid in facilitating a controlled conversation so that resolution can be attained and in record setting time.

The Decision Model

❑ **Step One: The "S"** guides you to **stop** and **see** what the situation is (analyze what it is).

❑ **Step Two: The "T"** directs you to **think through** your analysis.

❑ **Step Three: The "O"** cautions against hasty decisions and directs you to **organize** your **options** (plural) for dealing with "S."

❑ **Step Four: The "P"** demands that you now **pick** the most viable option and implement it (**proceed**) for the action plan.

You can write these letters out on a piece of paper, chalkboard or easel to guide group conversations as well, and avoid the negative dialogue and terrorists that can derail a meeting or team effectiveness!

CYA

Y ou have had this experience! Or have you?

You felt instinctively that things were not going the way they should, that it would be smart to have back-up copies of correspondence and/or other information to cover your actions and the actions of others around you. The only problem is that even though you knew you should have, you didn't. When the negativity hit the fan, you had no documentation to backup your positions or documentation to protect yourself.

Technique #36 – CYA in the most comprehensive manner that you know how!

And, we all know that CYA stands for COVERING YOUR ACTIONS!

There are some very simple rules about Covering Your Actions. Do it!

If you are corresponding with someone on sensitive matters, keep copies. Consider sending copies to two or three other individuals related to the subject matter. This keeps the recipient of your correspondence in check (now you know what those letters "CC" at the bottom of a page mean).

If you are sending electronic mail or receiving electronic mail messages of sensitive matters that can come back to haunt you, make copies of these as well!

And, the most important rule of all ... KEEP THESE COPIES OFF-SITE AND NOT, FOR EXAMPLE, IN A FILE AT WORK. I have known a lot of people who have been wrongfully terminated and had no documentation to cover their actions and support their position. With the documentation saved off-site, they would have had the information and evidence necessary to be financially secure!

Letting Go

You have to know when to drop it and LET GO. Most people don't know when it is in their best interest to shut up and let go!

So, how do you determine when it is best to LET GO? Measure the facts!

Technique #37 – LETTING GO. It's easy to say and very difficult for most people to actually do!

To determine whether to LET GO or apply yourself to a negative situation or norm within an organization (work or home), on a scale of high to low, plot in your head or on a piece of paper two important measurements.

Plot the vertical axis line first and then the horizontal axis, to determine your best course of action. And then follow that course and don't change your course of action. Stick to it!

HIGH

What is the **Reality** that you can do anything about the negative issue/norm?	☐ Personal Agenda ☐ Drop It!	☐ Take Action ☐ Do Something
	☐ LET GO!	☐ It Matters ☐ Influence Others

LOW   If you could do something about the negative issue or **HIGH** norm, what would be the **real impact on change** for the positive?

Knowing when to "LET GO" is important to moving beyond negativity and toward a positive course of action.

Fogging
(i.e., distracting)

Switching the focus from one subject especially when that subject is negative – to another more productive course of discussion is the intent of FOGGING.

In essence, you switch the conversation from the negative context to another context with positive intent.

Technique #38 – FOGGING – deals with switching the context of one conversation to another!

It could sound like, "That is a good point, and in looking at (insert new subject matter)...."

Buying Time

Negative people love to push you for an immediate action plan or response. Many times it is your immediate response that aids the negative person in his pursuit of you.

In BUYING TIME, always ask yourself, "do I need to make an immediate decision here or respond immediately." If not, delay the final decision for later and allow yourself some reflective thought time.

Mega-negaholics and trained terrorists have learned to pressure you and cause you to do or say things that may otherwise not have been made or said. This, too, adds to the negative feelings between the parties involved.

***Technique #39 – BUYING TIME –
implies not allowing yourself to be
pressured into making decisions that
will ultimately add to negativity!***

If you find yourself being pressured for a decision and the added benefit of BUYING TIME would be to your advantage, then:

> ❑ Excuse yourself for the bathroom, most people would not deny you this venture. Once removed from the environment you

were in, clearer thinking can resume and allow you time to refocus your decision abilities.

❑ Ask to get input from others before making a decision. Immediately turn in the direction of those other people (telephone them, walk to get them, send an electronic mail message, etc.).

This technique is presented successfully by a colleague of mine, Ms. Lauree Olsen from Salt Lake City, Utah in her crises management workshops. Never allow yourself to be bullied into a decision that could have been made at a later date!

Trade Offs

Reduce competitive roles with negative people by remaining focused on the core objective and expressing your willingness to give and take some issues for resolution.

This can become a fast way to resolve a conflict by examining what the other party's wants or needs truly are and weighing them against what your true needs are.

Technique #40 – TRADE OFFS – directs you to guide the conversation looking for positive choices for them, which you can live with also!

An example might sound like this,

> ❏ "If you would rather not come in on Saturday and would prefer to come in earlier on Monday morning, any way we can take care of this work before the start of business on Monday is fine with me."

What you want is the work taken care of, and whether it can be done on Saturday or Monday doesn't matter to you. You are trading doing the work on Saturday for earlier on Monday, as long as all parties are in agreement.

Welcoming

Make it easy for negative news to be delivered to you and for negative individuals to address you. This may sound unusual, but remember that negative people love negative situations and anything which can escalate the negative.

Your approach is to do the opposite of what they are trained to expect when the negative one-two punch is delivered.

Technique #41 – WELCOMING. Invite the negative in a controlled manner!

Your intent here is to focus the conversation on the core subject matter and not allow yourself to get caught up in the negative tones of voice or subtle jabs that are made toward you.

An example might sound like this,

> ❑ **"I can appreciate your concern about ....**" Then you keep right on talking in the direction of the real issues as you see them. If you can conclude the conversation with a question which they have to address, even better.

> ❑ **"I can appreciate your patience...."** Then continue your conversation.

Pull Back

Sometimes the best approach deserves saying twice. Sometimes the best approach deserves saying twice!

When someone says something or implies something is negative, where they would normally expect you to go ballistic, don't. Better yet the only words from your mouth should be to solicit them to say it again.

The beauty here is that they hear themselves saying it the first time, then they don't get the response from you that they would expect. They will be hard pressed to say it quite the way they did the first time.

Technique #42 – PULL BACK – puts the pressure back on them!

It might sound like this,

> ❑ They have just said something with a negative connotation, you say, **"excuse me?"** This pulls them back, and typically they will now address the subject, minus the negative.

You can both focus on the real issues at hand, not the subtle or blatant negative jabs at one another!

Family Matters

O ne of what may be the oldest rules or techniques for staying out of negative situation deals with the family circle.

Technique #43 – FAMILY MATTERS – but out!

Remember the old adage of how best to participate in issues of family matters which do not directly involve you:

❏ Rule One. Stay out

❏ Rule Two. Reread rule one!

The Mississippi Count-Off

This technique is a classic! You may have to read it more than once to fully appreciate its impact and power.

When you were little and your parents told you to count to yourself by saying "One Mississippi, two Mississippi, three Mississippi, four Mississippi, five Mississippi, etc."

The point to this approach (technique) is that if your response comes so fast and so automatically at the receiving end of a negative comment or situation, you will inevitably say something to increase the negative or you'll say something that later you may wish you had said differently or not said at all.

Counting off in your head a sequence of one through five gives you the opportunity to put your emotions in check, regain conscious control. Now you will be able to proceed with a more rational and calm comment or action plan.

Technique #44 – THE MISSISSIPPI COUNT-OFF – your parents' voice whispering to you to pause before responding!

Chance rewards the prepared mind! In responding to negative people and negative situations, it is the focused mind that receives the spoils of victory.

Technology Talk

When you know you need to interact with a negative person (for communication or information exchange purposes), consider your other options.

Many times you may realize that the actual physical interaction between you and another person aren't required. You may recognize that, with some issues and with some people, what is really needed is to get information from them.

Technique #45 – TECHNOLOGY TALK!

Reduce the number of times that you may have to actually interact with others. Become better at TECHNOLOGY TALK.

An example,

> ❏ Leave messages, send messages through the telephone voice mail messaging systems or send an electronic mail message. Even use an independent third party to relay data.

For the times when you don't have to actually talk to the other person, become a better stu-

dent of TECHNOLOGY TALK and remove yourself from the environment of the negative and
limit your exposure to negative people.

Physical Destresser

S ometimes the best negativity busting medi- cine is to realign the physical energies in your body from heightened physical stress to lowered physical relaxation.

In most encounters with negative people or pro- longed interaction with them on tasks with high levels of stress or negativity, there is the need to channel your physical energies from the state of tension towards a more relaxed, controlled and focused state.

One technique that allows you to channel ener- gies from negative to positive deals with realigning your physiology – forced tensors.

Technique #46 – PHYSICAL DESTRESSER – a realignment of your physiology from a tension state to a quiet and more relaxed state is necessary!

This is simple to explain, yet hard to have the self-discipline to perform,

> ❏ **Step One**, stop everything you are do- ing and simply start counting to yourself at a slow rate, numbers one through ten.

❑ **Step Two**, as you sit there in your seat or stand in line (etc.), you make a fist and curl your toes. Tighten up your arms and legs as tight as you can make them. You do this slowly as you count one through five.

❑ **Step Three**, repetition is the secret here. As you count one through five you tighten. Pause at five and then as you continue counting six through ten, you relax the limbs, hands and toes. Then repeat this process five to ten times. The final outcome is a leveling of your energy and a quieter mind. You are more relaxed and thus focus can return to you.

Deep Breathing Destresser

S o you have finally reached the boiling over point with a situation or individual. Don't explode, instead take a d-e-e-p b-r-e-a-t-h!

While it might make you feel temporarily good to blowup, it usually results in increased animosity, tension and more negativity. To regain mental focus and not lose physical control, change your breathing patterns to increase the oxygen flow through your system – resulting in a lowering of your heart rate and internal pace.

Technique #47 – DEEP BREATHING DESTRESSER – an immediate change in your breathing pattern to allow for an immediate internal calming effect!

Simple to explain, yet hard to have the self discipline to perform. The process,

> ❑ **Step One**, stop everything you are doing and simply start counting to yourself at a slow rate, numbers one through ten.

> ❑ **Step Two**, as you sit there in your seat or stand in line (etc.), you take in a deep whole breath. You do this slowly as you

count one through five and fill your en-
tire insides full with air.

❑ **Step Three**, repetition is the secret
here. As you count one through five you
inhale. Pause at five, hold the breath for
few seconds, and, then as you continue
counting six through ten, you exhale.

Then repeat this process five to ten times. The
final outcome is a leveling of your energy and a
quieter mind, due to a slowing down of your self-
induced hyper-ventilation and induced anxiety.

Mental Vacation Destresser

So you have finally reached the boiling over point with a situation or individual, and you are trying to apply the forced tensors and deep breathing techniques, but there still seems to be something missing. Add a mental time-out to the technique line-up as well!

The objective is simple. Isolate yourself temporarily from the negative thing which is causing your stress (a few seconds will work and the longer you can give yourself the better!). Don't light up a cigarette or open a can of soda (as most of those are stimulants, NOT relaxants).

Technique #48 – MENTAL VACATION DESTRESSER. Change your thinking process from the stressors to something, anything that stimulates relaxing and positive mental imagery!

Simple to explain, yet hard to have the self discipline to perform. The process,

> ❏ **Step One**, stop everything you are doing and close your eyes. Pull up a mental picture of something, anything, anyone else that is associated in your minds' eye with a positive.

❑ **Step Two**, as you sit there in your seat or stand in line (etc.), you take this new imagery and let the mental video tape roll. Re-experience all of the positives associated with that video tape.

❑ **Step Three**, repetition is the secret here. Keep playing the tape until you feel yourself more in control and less anxious and stressed.

Or What?

Have we missed an obvious technique that you find works for you? If so, then send your technique, with a detailed explanation of what it is and how to use it to us.

If we use your idea in our next printing, you will receive complimentary copies, and a free library of all the author's available self-development and professional resources!

Technique #49 – ... OR WHAT?

Simple to explain, let us know. The process,

❏ **Step One**, send your technique and explanation to JMI Publishing. c/o **ENOUGH ALREADY!** JMI®, Inc., P.O. Box 701918, Tulsa, Oklahoma, 74170-1918. Or, fax it Tollfree to 1-877-90-MAGEE.

❏ **Step Two**, make sure to include your name, address and daytime phone number for contact.

Move!!!

E**nough already!**

You have tried every conceivable technique known to the educated and even under-educated world. There is no human sign of change on the horizon and no matter what you do, you feel confident that there will be no change for the positive.

Well, guess what? You have just told yourself what the next course of action must be. MOVE!

Technique #50 – MOVE!

The question that needs to resonate within you is, "Do I want to be in the same position with the same questions before me in six months?" If the answer is no, then MOVE!

You can MOVE in a lot of directions. The process,

> ❏ **Step One**, remain in the geography but move (change) your specific location to limit exposure, interaction and contact with the negative situations or people.

> ❏ **Step Two.** Better yet, make a horizontal move in a work environment to get your sanity back and distance yourself

from the situations or people that cause you such internal grief.

❏ **Step Three.** Better yet, move completely out of the geography where all of the negative influencers are. Maybe, far enough away that they can't get to you so easily, yet close enough that if, for some reason, you want to or need to get back, it is doable!

Remember, negative needs an audience and if you're not there, it will move on and terrorize someone else.

About the Author

Jeffrey L. Magee, Ph.D./CMC/PDM

• • • • •

A recognized authority, with explosive ideas, a style that captivates audiences and an energy level that is contagious, Jeff heads up his own management training group.

He presents more than 200 keynote and educational seminars each year – internationally and repeatedly in all 50 states. **Jeff's programs take you from where you are, to where you must be for success!** Jeff works with clients ranging from Fortune 100 to government agencies to both profit and not-for-profit based organizations. He's presented before more than 500,000 people through on-site seminars, keynotes and public appearances with civic organizations, and chamber of commerce sponsored symposiums!

Since the age of 15, Jeff has learned about business and people up-close and personal. His first venture in business advertising with *Cherry Blossoms Advertising*, was purchased by a major business while in high school. After ten years as an investigative business writer for newspapers, he went back into the business world. At age 24, Jeff was recognized by *American Home Products, Inc.* (a Fortune 500 firm) as their top salesman in the nation and was promoted to a Territory Manager. In 1988 his territory was recognized as the number three territory in America – a month later he experienced corporate down-sizing and was let go! He prevailed...and was employed in less than 24 hours.

Jeff went on to set sales and marketing records as a sales associate and later as the Vice President for *Target Marketing, Inc.* by day, while at the same time becoming the youngest certified sales instructor internationally for *Dale Carnegie® Seminars* by age 27 at night. In 1991, after experiencing down-sizing for the second time, he started his own publishing, training and organizational development firm – **JEFF MAGEE INTERNATIONAL®**.

Along the way he has had **more than 200 articles published,** earned a bachelors degree in Mass Communication and Political Science, a Masters Certification as a Professional Direct Marketer (**PDM**) and his Ph.D. in Psychology. And, he is a Certified Management Consultant (**CMC**) by The Institute of Management Consultants in New York City.

He has written **five hit selling books**, produced three success oriented audio tape series, **anchored two team building and management effectiveness training videos** (which are sold internationally by – *CareerTrack® Seminars* and *SkillPath® Seminars, Inc.*, respectfully), **serves as Publisher** of *PERFORMANCE®* magazine, and **serves/served on** the Boards of Directors for a leading Midwest University, a national Fraternity, civic organizations and several arts groups.

Proof that success can be attained at any level, at any age and under any situation, Magee has **MAPS**© that work!

For More Information Contact:

JEFF MAGEE INTERNATIONAL®
On-Site Information/Scheduling
Tollfree 1-877-90-MAGEE
P. O. Box 701918
Tulsa, OK 74170-1918
www.jeffmageeintl.com

Jeff Magee

PRODUCT ORDER FORM

Individual Title	Qty	Amount
Yield Management — Book .... $27.95 The Leadership Alternative for Performance and Net Profit Improvement		
The Leadership Alternative — Book .... $19.95 9 Steps to High Impact Leadership		
Power Charged For Life — Book .... $12.95 Systems for Designing a Championship Attitude		
Enough Already! — Book .... $12.95 50 Ways to Deal With, Manage and Eliminate Negativity		
Promoting Yourself In The Workplace — Audio ..... $15.95 How to Quietly Help Yourself By Helping Others		
Coaching and Teambuilding Skills — Audio .... $19.95 For Managers & Supervisers		
Coaching and Teambuilding Skills — Video .... $139.95 For Managers & Supervisers		
	Sub Total	
No tax, no shipping charges for direct purchase orders	TOTAL	

Jeff Magee International
P.O.Box 701918 • Tulsa OK 74170-1918

Tollfree: 1-877-90-MAGEE

On the web at: www.jeffmageeintl.com

Name _____ Date _____

Company _____

Street Address _____

City/Province _____ State _____

Zip/Postal Code _____ Country _____ Day Phone _____

☐ **YES** — *Please send me information on Jeff Magee's speaking services.*

☐ CHECK or ☐ CREDIT CARD

☐ VISA ☐ MC | Card No. / / / / / / / / / / / / / / / /

Exp. date _____ Signature _____

119